Ten P~
about Nc

C000044105

ex libris

Candlestick Press

Published by:
Candlestick Press,
Diversity House, 72 Nottingham Road, Arnold, Nottingham NG5 6LF
www.candlestickpress.co.uk

Design, typesetting, print and production by Diversity Creative
Marketing Solutions Ltd., www.diversity.agency

Selection and Introduction © John Lucas, 2015

Cover illustration © Sarah Kirby, www.sarahkirby.co.uk, 2015

© Candlestick Press, 2015

ISBN 978 1 907598 35 7

Acknowledgements:
Our thanks to John Lucas for selecting these poems about Nottingham,
our home city. Thanks are also due to Wayne Burrows for permission
to reprint 'The Second Time as Farce' from *Black Glass: New
and Selected Poems* (Shoestring Press, 2015); Derrick Buttress for
'Welcome to the Bike Factory' from *Welcome to the Bike Factory*
(Shoestring Press, 2014); Shoestring Press for Joan Downar, 'War Jaw'
from *Various Returns: A Selection of Posthumous Poems*, ed. Michael
Payne (Shoestring Press, 2014); Rosie Garner for 'Football on Vernon
Park' from *The Rain Diaries* (Salt Publishing, 2010); Cathy Grindrod
for 'Crocus Fields' from *The Sky, Head On* (Shoestring Press, 2009);
Deborah Tyler-Bennett for 'Nottingham Evening Post: Valentine's Day,
1914' from *Clark Gable in Mansfield: Selected Poems* (Rotherham:
King's England Press, 2003) reprinted in *Take Five* (Shoestring Press,
2003). Thanks also to the Estate of Vernon Scannell for permission
to reprint 'Autobiographical Note' from *Vernon Scannell, Collected
Poems 1950 – 1993* (Faber, 2010).

Where poets are no longer living, their dates are given.

Contents

Introduction

As the legend of Robin Hood indicates, Nottingham's fame long pre-dates the coming of the Industrial Revolution. In this it is unlike most other large cities of the English midlands and north. And as the fate of its twice-burnt castle also indicates, the city has always been associated with rebelliousness. At the outset of the English civil war, Charles I's forces raised the royal standard over the city. But Cromwell's forces drove them out.... Throughout the county men fought on both sides and on both sides died. Hence the measured cost-reckoning of Joan Downar's 'War Jaw'.

Perhaps sobriety helped the Commonwealth cause, but in the eighteenth century brewing became an important industry, and the ballad on Nottingham Ale is one of several written in praise of a drink whose quality is often ascribed to the waters of what Hotspur in Shakespeare's *Henry IV, Part I* calls "the smug and silver Trent". ("Smug" = "smooth".)

But ale, which can make men rebellious, had its decriers, including the poet Henry Kirke White (1785 – 1806) who, looking across from the heights of his native village, Clifton, sees the growing city where "manufacture taints the ambient skies", and imagines the pale mechanic leaving his loom in order to pursue "The stated course of customary sin" – i.e. getting drunk.

Not far from the Lace Market, where the lace industry throve, Market Square stands at the city's centre. In the early 1840s the writer William Howitt, who with his more talented wife, Mary, had an apothecary's shop at the corner of the square, walked most mornings through crocus fields in order to bathe in the Trent. Cathy Grindrod's 'The Crocus Gatherers' takes its cue from a painting, now in the city's Castle Museum, which depicts these long gone fields, though a present-day Crocus Street provides the dusty echo of rural life that once abutted the city.

The mining industry has also gone, but its importance to city and surrounding country is sardonically assessed in Deborah Tyler-Bennett's 'Nottingham Evening Post: Valentine's Day, 1914', while D. H. Lawrence's ballad-style narrative, 'A Collier's Wife', uses dialect and idiom to keep wonderfully alive local habits of speech.

By the mid-1930s, some twenty years after Lawrence's poem was written, Nottingham possessed no fewer than thirty-nine cinemas, and one of them, the Beeston Essoldo, became the dream palace where in 'Autobiography' Vernon Scannell recalls pre-war Saturday mornings of early boyhood. Rosie Garner's 'Football on Vernon Park' takes for its subject a later generation of boys; and still older boys, finished with school, are made 'Welcome to the Bike Factory' in Derrick Buttress's laconic account of employment at one time taken for granted by thousands of local youths, among them Alan Sillitoe's Arthur Seaton.

It's doubtful whether Seaton, a loner, would have been one of the street celebrants recorded in Wayne Burrows' 'The Second Time as Farce', which directs a quizzical gaze at contemporary city revellers. Yet the poem also celebrates a comic exuberance discoverable in city life. Beneath its ambient air, and 'Between folk memory, amnesia and marketing', an instinctive rebelliousness may stir... .

John Lucas, Beeston

Welcome to the Bike Factory

We will begin with the history of the Company,
how six artisans of the old school
sweated over the manipulation of steel
until even their skill could not keep pace,
how the genius with an eye on the future
broke down the art into function,
the skill into units of wealth
that paid ten thousand numbers
clocking on, clocking off

followed by advice

on how not to get crushed, cut or torn,
what to do if you find a finger missing,
(what to do with the missing finger)
how to deal with shock, electrocution,
broken foot bones and skin disease
(through no fault of ours)
what to say to the man with the tang
of a file thrust through his wrist
and other information
relevant to your survival:

your point of departure
your chance of promotion
what we will pay you
what it will cost you

after which we will convey you
to the assembly line
to the assembly line
to the assembly line

Derrick Buttress

Nottingham Ale

Fair Venus, the goddess of beauty and love,
   Arose from the froth which swam on the sea:
Minerva leapt out of the *cranium* of Jove,
   A coy sullen slut, as most authors agree;
Bold Bacchus, they tell us, the prince of good fellows,
   Was a natural son – pray attend to my tale;
But they that thus chatter, mistake quite the matter –
   He sprang from a barrel of Nottingham ale;
   Nottingham ale, boys, Nottingham ale;
   No liquor on earth like Nottingham ale!

And having survey'd well the cask whence he sprung,
   For want of more liquor, low-spirited grew;
He mounted astride, set himself on the bung,
   And away to the gods and the goddesses flew;
But, when he look'd down, and saw the fair town,
   To pay it due honours, not likely to fail;
He swore that on earth, 'twas the place of his birth,
   And the best – and no liquor like Nottingham ale,
   Nottingham ale, boys, Nottingham ale;
   No liquor on earth like Nottingham ale!

Ye bishops and deacons, priests, curates, and vicars,
   When once you have tasted you'll own it is true,
That Nottingham ale is the best of all liquors;
   And who understands the good creature like you?
It expels every vapour – saves pen, ink, and paper;
   And when you're disposed from the pulpit to rail,
'Twill open your throats – you may preach without notes
   When inspired with a bumper of Nottingham ale.
   Nottingham ale, boys, Nottingham ale;
   No liquor on earth like Nottingham ale!

Ye doctors, who more execution have done
  With powder and bolus, with potion and pill,
Than hangman with halter, or soldier with gun,
  Than miser with famine, or lawyer with quill;
To dispatch us the quicker, you forbid us malt liquor,
  Till our bodies consume, and our faces grow pale;
But mind it, what pleases, and cures all diseases,
  Is a comforting dose of good Nottingham ale!
  Nottingham ale, boys, Nottingham ale;
  No liquor on earth like Nottingham ale!

Ye poets who brag of the Helicon brook,
  The nectar of gods, and the juice of the vine;
You say none can write well, except they invoke
  The friendly assistance of one of the *nine*;
Here's liquor surpasses the streams of Parnassus,
  The nectar ambrosia, on which gods regale;
Experience will show it, nought makes a good poet
  Like *quantum sufficit* of Nottingham ale!
  Nottingham ale, boys, Nottingham ale;
  No liquor on earth like Nottingham ale!

'Mr Gemthorpe' (written pre-1815)

From **Clifton Grove**

Now, when the rustic wears the social smile,
Released from day and its attendant toil,
And draws his household round their evening fire,
And tells the oft told tales that never tire;
Or, where the town's blue turrets dimly rise,
And manufacture taints the ambient skies,
The pale mechanic leaves the labouring loom,
The air-pent hold, the pestilential room,
And rushes out, impatient to begin
The stated course of customary sin:
Now, now my solitary way I bend
Where solemn groves in awful state impend:
And cliffs, that boldly rise above the plain,
Bespeak bless'd Clifton! Thy sublime domain.
Here lonely wandering o'er the sylvan bower,
I come to pass the meditative hour;
To bid awhile the strife of passion cease,
And woo the calms of solitude and peace.

Henry Kirke White (1785 – 1806)

The Crocus Gatherers, Nottingham Meadows

after the painting by Samuel William Oscroft in Nottingham Castle Museum

The crocus gatherers have come,
as they have always come,
since Zeus and Hera
made love so passionate
a whole bank burst
with those first blooms –
egg-yolk yellow, white,
royal velvet purple,
petals hollering –

as once they came
to gather flowers for saffron,
four thousand orange stigmas
for one pure ounce –
for illuminating missals,
sweet flavourings,
liquors for the rich,

and still they come.
Look, they have reached
the last patch,
filling their hands with Spring.

Cathy Grindrod

A Collier's Wife

Somebody's knocking at the door
    Mother, come down and see,
– I's think it's nobbut a beggar,
    Say, I'm busy.

It's not a beggar, mother, – hark
    How hard he knocks...
– Eh, th'art a mard-'arsed kid,
    'E'll gi'e thee socks!

Shout an' ax what 'e wants,
    I canna come down.
– 'E says 'Is it Arthur Holliday's?'
    Say 'Yes,' tha clown.

'E says, 'Tell your mother as 'er mester's
    Got hurt i' th' pit.'
What – oh my sirs, 'e never says that,
    That's niver it.

Come out o' the way an' let me see,
    Eh, there's no peace!
An stop thy scraightin', childt,
    Do shut thy face.

'Your mester's 'ad an accident,
    An' they're ta'ein 'im i' th' ambulance
To Nottingham,' – Eh dear o' me
    If 'e's not a man for mischance!

Wheers he hurt this time, lad?
– I dunna know,
They on'y towd me it wor bad –
    It would be so!

Eh, what a man! – an' that cobbly road,
    They'll jolt him a'most to death,
I'm sure he's in for some trouble
    Nigh every time he takes breath.

Out o' my way, childt – dear o' me, where
    Have I put his clean stockings and shirt;
Goodness knows if they'll be able
    To take off his pit dirt.

An' what a moan he'll make – there niver
    Was such a man for a fuss
If anything ailed him – at any rate
    I shan't have him to nuss.

I do hope it's not very bad!
    Eh, what a shame it seems
As some should ha'e hardly a smite o'trouble
    An' others has reams.

It's a shame as 'e should be knocked about
    Like this, I'm sure it is!
He's had twenty accidents, if he's had one;
    Owt bad, an' it's his.

There's one thing, we'll have peace for a bit,
    Thank Heaven for a peaceful house;
An' there's compensation, sin' it's accident,
    An' club money – I nedn't grouse.

An' a fork an' a spoon he'll want, an' what else;
    I s'll never catch that train –
What a traipse it is if a man gets hurt –
    I s'd think he'll get right again.

D. H. Lawrence (1885 – 1930)

Nottingham Evening Post, Valentine's Day, 1914

for Jack, Doris, and my Great Grandfather, Joseph Lawrence

Fifty lines on how King George may visit
the Duke of Portland and attend the hunt,
and thirty on a bride-to-be named Blisset
whose name on marriage will be Lady Blunt.
Twelve for stories full of postcard humour,
someone in Beeston swallowed her false teeth,
a window-cleaner caught a glimpse of bloomer
and was mistaken for a petty thief.
Another fifty-one detailing billiards,
a further thirty on the boxing ring,
or fancy dress with courtiers dressed as Hilliards,
and ten on hats that are the latest thing.
Four on Great Grandad, working at his stall,
killed at just thirty-six by pit roof fall.

Deborah Tyler-Bennett

War Jaw

Whose leg is this? Dear chap,
I think it must be mine
and this would be your hand.
An unfortunate mishap
to be thus met, we a small band
from Willoughby Field,
our fine plumes crushed, you
mopping up from Cromwell's line.

Those Costock ploughmen thrust
us willy-nilly deep
outside the church's wall.
Forgive me, but I must
presume this gourd to be your skull.
Or is it mine? I keep
remembering our encounter, and trust
you manage sleep.

They call this place the War Hill
or the Worrill, and it's food
for thought for innocents
whose only battles are the ill
they bear their neighbours. Whence
think you, come these jaw-bones, blood
adhering, shattered still, and disengaged for good?

Joan Downar (1930 – 1996)

Note: In the 1880s some bones disinterred from outside Costock church wall
were found to be those of men who had apparently been killed in a minor
skirmish between royalists and parliamentarians on a nearby hill, still then
called the Worrill. The battle of Willoughby Field had occurred nearby in 1648
in which the cavaliers were crushed by Colonel Rossiter. Joan Downar was
asked in 1992 to write a poem commemorating the 250th anniversary of the
outbreak of the Civil War.

Autobiographical Note

Beeston, the place, near Nottingham:
We lived there for three years or so.
Each Saturday at two-o'clock
We queued up for the matinée,
All the kids for streets around
With snotty noses, giant caps,
Cut down coats and heavy boots,
The natural enemies of cops
And schoolteachers. Profane and hoarse
We scrambled, yelled and fought until
The Picture Palace opened up
And we, like Hamelin children, forced
Our bony way into the hall.
That much is easy to recall;
Also the reek of chewing-gum,
Gob-stoppers and liquorice,
But of the flickering myths themselves
Not much remains. The hero was
A milky wide-brimmed hat, a shape
Astride the arched white stallion;
The villain's horse and hat were black.
Disbelief did not exist
And laundered virtue always won
With quicker gun and harder fist,
And all of us applauded it.
Yet I remember moments when
In solitude I'd find myself
Brooding on the sooty man,
The bristling villain, who could move
Imagination in a way
The well-shaved hero never could,
And even warm the nervous heart
With something oddly close to love.

Vernon Scannell (1922 – 2007)

Football on Vernon Park

A patient man,
he cups his hand against the wind,
lights his fag as the game gets underway.
Nods, *they'll shape up nice this year,*
the under eights.

With a lift of his arm and a call,
like a shepherd signalling his dogs,
he'll nudge a winger back in place,
picks out the sub,
sets him running down the field;
all the way,
if you want to play, you'll run.
He pinches off his fag and watches everything,
good lad, well done.

Across the pitch,
the knot of parents,
buggies, barking dogs.
Breath steaming for the first time this year,
trees leaning in to the end of summer.

And the boys standing
almost in their places,
hands on hips, rucked-up sleeves
that dangle back below their waists
as soon as they begin to run,
deadly serious, knowing the rules
and sticking to them.

You can see, in their cool appraisal of their game,
their shrugging acceptance of missed goals,
like shadows standing behind them,
the men they'll grow into.
He watches from the centre,
almost smiles, sees them now.

Rosie Garner

The Second Time as Farce

The men in orange and yellow striped lycra tights,
the men in fishnet stockings and white silk suspender belts,
are calling to the women wearing pink lace fairy wings,
the women wearing yellow *San Diego* cheerleader vests,

and the men in bottle-blonde Marilyn Monroe wigs,
the boys in animal masks borrowed from *The Wicker Man,*
are calling to the women wearing green leather basques,
the girls in cut-off denim shorts and cowboy boots,

and the men dressed in football shirts and velour jester hats,
the men dressed as Crockett and Tubbs from *Miami Vice,*
are calling to the women wearing *Blade Runner* retro-1940s hair,
wearing pencil skirts, red lipstick, scarlet fingernails,

and the men dressed as Batman and Robin, as Adam West and
Burt Ward,
the men in clown suits, or wearing Primark suits and ties,
are calling to the women in red-framed plastic spectacles
whose hair is inflamed to *Dallas* heights or roughly dyed,

and the man wearing nothing but his blue cotton boxer shorts,
the men in gimp masks and burkhas and Biblical robes,
are calling to the women dressed as nurses and chambermaids,
the girl dressed as someone I think I met, once, back in nineteen
eighty-six,

and the man in a rubber *Point Break* Richard Nixon mask,
the men in *Matrix* coats, in wide-brimmed black leather hats,
are calling to the women dressed in T-shirts that read:
'Frankie Says...',
dressed as Toyah, Siouxsie Sioux and Cruella de Ville,

and the music that drifts from the windows of all the pubs
is by Eurythmics, by Whitney Houston and Adam Ant,
and the tinny music playing on every mobile phone
is by Grandmaster Flash, Five Star, The Smiths and Culture Club,

and they keep coming, gathered in groups of four or six,
to the epicentre of this Wednesday night, to Market Square,
to the open doors of Yates's, the two-for-one Jagerbomb
                                                    carpet-bars,
the cocktail lounge where nothing's changed since 1993,

and in all this, between folk memory, amnesia and marketing,
the men in orange and yellow striped lycra tights
and the men in fishnet stockings and silk suspender belts
are still calling to the women wearing pink lace fairy wings.

Wayne Burrows

John Lucas is a distinguished poet, academic and publisher. His scholarly and critical works include studies of Charles Dickens, John Clare, Ivor Gurney and several books on English poetry. Among his recent publications are *A Brief History of Whistling* (with Allan Chatburn), *The Awkward Squad: Rebels in English Cricket* and *Portable Property: Poems.* He is Professor Emeritus at the Universities of Loughborough and Nottingham Trent and lives in Nottingham.